Divine Artistry

By

Yvonne Lyons

authorHOUSE®

To Margaret
God Bless.
Yvonne Lyons
2016

AuthorHouse™ UK Ltd.
500 Avebury Boulevard
Central Milton Keynes, MK9 2BE
www.authorhouse.co.uk
Phone: 08001974150

First published by AuthorHouse 9/16/2009

ISBN: 978-1-4389-9037-8 (sc)

This book is printed on acid-free paper.

About The Author

Yvonne Lyons was born in Belfast, but has lived in Carrickfergus for the past twenty years.

She is a very talented writer and has a great appreciation of nature and this is expressed through her inspirational poems.

An accomplished musician, with a keen interest in choral music, she belongs to the singing group 'Trio Cantabile' and has written words and music for many inspirational songs which the group has performed, giving concerts in theatres, concert halls, and many other venues.

Throughout the years her poetry books, written for Action Cancer and Clic Sargent Cancer Care for Children, have raised around £12,000 for these charities. Because of this achievement she was nominated for the television programme 'Making a Difference'.

An identical twin, she has a very close relationship with her sister Iris, they are so alike and are always together. Her husband Clifford is also a twin. She has three grown-up children, Dawn, Graham and Alan, and two lovely little grandchildren, Jack and Cara.

Yvonne's book of inspirational verse 'Divine Artistry' re-affirms belief in all the important aspects of life. Take time to read between the lines and you will find spiritual blessing too.

Preface

The title of my book 'Divine Artistry' is inspired by God's handiwork as I view the wonder and the beauty of nature. These poems are written with spiritual feeling and expression and bring God's blessing to people in all walks of life.

I have a great love of music and find divine inspiration in being able to express my inner feelings as I share each musical moment with God.

It has also been a great privilege and blessing to bring into focus people less fortunate than myself. This has been a very humbling experience.

I think you would agree that God is also present on the humorous side of life.

The Glens of Antrim, Causeway Coast, and the famous Carrickfergus Castle are very dear to my heart and all have pride of place.

There are various children's poems, included are childhood memories and I have given you an insight into the life of identical twins.

But the spiritual poems are the most poignant. Especially those telling the wonderful stories of Easter and Christmas. I am aware that the section on Heaven is very emotional, but God is closest to those who have to bear sorrow and pain and these will mean so much to many people who are suffering, bringing them comfort and hope for the future.

As you journey through life, take time to appreciate the beauty of the earth which God has crowned with glory and honour.

Yvonne Lyons

Foreword

I am delighted and honoured to be invited to write the foreword to this latest addition to Yvonne's library of inspired poems.

Many readers of Yvonne's earlier works have gained strength and encouragement from the verses which have flowed from her pen and I know that this new, somewhat larger volume will add to that success. In a very practical way, too, the funds raised through these publications have brought comfort to many who have been suffering in various ways.

I trust we can all identify with the truths captured in these poems, reminding us of the fundamentals of our Christian faith – like the miracle of Christmas and the unique sacrifice of the first Easter - and the 'Divine Artistry' we enjoy every day as we contemplate the lilies of the field or the countless stars above our heads at night.

I trust you will revert regularly to this book and draw freely on the rich observations and truths which Yvonne has been inspired and privileged to make available to her widening audience.

I wish Yvonne and this new anthology every success.

ALDERMAN PATRICIA McKINNEY
Mayor of Carrickfergus

Contents

Divine Artistry..1
Whispers from Heaven 2
The Miracle 3
St. Gobbans God's Smallest Dwelling Place 4

Spring

The Return of Spring 6
God's Holy Spring-Clean...7
Glenariff...8
The Lark Ascending...9
Carrickfergus Castle 10
Scenes of Antrim 11
Where Eagles Dare...12
Psalm 121...13
The Sermon on the Mount 14
The Beatitudes 15

Easter

Consider the Lilies 17
Was it for Me?..18
Calvary's Road 19
The Greatest Love Story 20
Doubting Thomas 21
The Love of Mary Magdalene 22
Calvary to Heaven 23
No Greater Love...24
The Answer...25
I Will Never Leave the Heart That Loves Me 26
Communion...27

Summer

Summer Midnight..29
The Sunflower...30
Evergreen 31
The Rose 32
Down by the Watermill..33

Autumn

Autumn Unawares 35
Harvest 36

The Power of Nature

The Power of Nature 38
Braving the Storm 39
Galilean Memories..40

Winter

Silent Worship 42
Sky Scenes 43
Wonders of Winter..44
November Magic..45

Christmas

God's Miracle Divine...47
Christmas Glory 48
From Bethlehem to Calvary...49
God's Message in the Snow 50
The Promise of Salvation 51
God's Heavenly Miracle...52

New Year

The Circle of Life..54
Millennium Worship 55

The New Jerusalem

Zion's River 57
The New Jerusalem 58

Music

Music 60
Upon Piano Keys 61
The Music Man's Song 62
Midnight Nocturne 63
Song without Words 64
Lonesome Melody 65
In Touch With God 66
A Blessing In Song from Ballyclare Male Choir 67
Waterfall Music 68
A Glimpse of God 69

Children's Poems

New-Born Love 71
The Gift of a Child 72
Do You Believe in Angels? 73
A Daisy for Mum 74
Cradle Love 75
How Much Does Love Cost? 76
Mr. Wonderful! 77
The Greatest Gift 78
Heaven's Embrace 79
Mischief Maker 80
Childhood Memories 81

Heaven

Mobile Heaven 83
He Holds the Future 84
Face to Face 85
Between the two of us 86
Broken Wings 87

Sea Pictures of Heaven 88
Just Beyond Your Tears 89
My Eternal Dream 90
Heaven's Dwelling Place 91
Sunrise Road 92
The In-between 93
God's All Revealing Light 94
Tapestry of Paradise 95
Conversion 96

Prayer

Wedding Prayer 98
Love's Fulfilment 99
One Moment! 100

Irish Poems

Erin's Isle 102
Vision by Moonlight 103
Faerie Dance 104

Other

God's Windows 106
A Mother's Love 107
Making a Difference 108
Loneliness 109
Two Hearts as One 110
Imprints 111
The Woman of the Well 112
He Touched My Soul 113

Divine Artistry

A garden is the Heavenly Artist's canvas,
Where He paints the living colours of the earth,
For God alone knows all of nature's secrets,
Capturing there the wonder of re-birth.

No artistry can re-invent God's palette,
Or breathe His 'breath of life' upon each scene,
As the first snowdrop's velvet petals are unfolding,
Embraced by frosted leaves of dabbled green.

And who can paint the butterfly that trembles,
With wings of gossamer upon the rose?
As we hold dew-kissed blossoms in our fingers,
Her fragrant scent God's artistry will disclose.

No masterpiece can imitate a heartbeat,
Throbbing within a tiny robin's breast,
Or the blackbird's song as day is dawning,
Or leafy trees the sighing winds caress.

The floral blossoms, nurtured by the sunshine,
In beauty grow by God's eternal plan,
By nature dressed in summer's favourite colours,
Perfection touched by God's almighty hand.

The artists of this world may paint a picture,
Inspired by inner vision and design,
But they will never re-create a garden,
To rival heaven's artistry divine.

Whispers from Heaven

As the early morn awakens, my Creator speaks to me,
And together we begin another day,
First I hear a 'Heavenly Whisper', and then His smile I see,
As the sunlight chases all the clouds away.

I listen to God speaking as I hear the Blackbird's song,
Her reverie is lingering on the breeze,
Enchantingly her love-call greets the summer morn,
Echoing 'Heavenly Whispers' through the trees.

And I can see God laughing as little children play,
Each single one is precious in His sight,
Engagingly He talks with them to pass the time away,
As I hear His 'Heavenly Whisper' of delight.

And in the hush of evening He reveals His 'Heavenly Chords',
As in classic mood He plays a melody,
These 'spiritual moments' only I can share with God,
As I hear His 'Heavenly Music' speak to me.

And then before the sunset, upon an age-ed face,
The beauty of the 'Smile of God' I see,
There I find His 'inner holiness' perfected in grace,
And I know God's 'Heavenly Whispers' speak to me.

The Miracle

I lifted up my heart unto the Lord
And found a miracle,
He offered unto me His saving grace
It was a miracle,
The answers to life's problems that I sought,
I could not find until
I lifted up my heart unto the Lord,
And found a miracle.

He took my life, and from that moment on
He wrought a miracle,
And with his wondrous gift of peace divine,
My heart and soul did fill,
And underneath the shadow of his wings,
I'll shelter from all ill,
For when I lifted up my heart to God,
He wrought a miracle.

Because my Saviour died on Calvary's cross,
For all humanity,
Forgiveness and redeeming grace is mine,
For all eternity,
Upon the heavenly countenance of God,
The light of love I'll see,
Because the Lord of Miracles is mine,
And He has pardoned me.

*God has given us all gifts. The greatest gift of all is love. If you dedicate your
gift to God he can make something beautiful of your life*

─────────────── 𝒴 ───────────────

St. Gobbans
God's Smallest Dwelling Place

By the scenic coast of Antrim
You'll find God's Dwelling Place,
So simple in her beauty -
And yet so fair of face,
Port Braddan is her sanctuary,
For years she's nestled there,
She watches o'er the fishing port,
Protected by God's care.

Where seagulls fly on sacred wings,
Beside the Atlantic shore,
She waits to welcome everyone
Who enters through her door,
And language is no barrier -
God understands each prayer,
For many friends from foreign lands,
Have found a refuge there.

So tiny is this little church,
And yet so big her heart,
For somehow you belong to her,
And you cannot depart
From the presence of this sanctuary
Of serenity and love,
Where you shared a 'Close Encounter'
With God in Heaven above.

*Port Braddan is a lovely little seaside village on the
Causeway Coast and this is the smallest church in
the world.*

Spring

The Return of Spring

Winter is lost in silent reverie -
As the first snowdrop's silver frosted petals,
Fragile and beautiful,
Melt like jewelled teardrops
Upon the face of the earth,
Wakened by the whispering breath of spring,
The crickets and bees with trembling wings
Embrace a world of unfolding beauty,
Drinking from freshly showered daffodils,
And seduced by sweet scented lilacs,
The blackbird sings in early expectancy,
With notes of purity, beautiful and true,
Warmed by the sun -
Suddenly the earth is infused
With wondrous colours of delicate perfection,
Bathed in creation's glory
The world looks on in silent worship,
And God is in his heaven.

God's Holy Spring-Clean

It's springtime up in Heaven, and because the weather's fine,
The Lord hangs out the snow-white clouds like washing on a line,
And then he sends a morning breeze so that they may tumbledry,
So fleecy and so fluffy as they blow across the sky.

He takes another look around and sees a bit of dust
Has gathered on the Angel Wings, to clean them is a must!
And when the job is finished, He asks the sun to shine,
And show up any little bits that He has left behind.

He's really very busy getting ready for the spring,
And a little bit of thunder is a sign He's hoovering!
In His 'House of Many Mansions' it's really quite a task,
For in order to complete the job, He has to work quite fast!

And when He's finished upstairs, He looks down upon the earth,
Then decides to send some April showers so that it may have
'new birth'.
The springtime flowers lift up their heads turned crimson, blue
and gold,
And the fleecy clouds all dance with joy as they the sight behold!

And He tells us all to waken up for 'springtime' is about,
Then everybody cleans their houses outside-in and inside-out!
We tidy up the garden, and we fertilize the ground,
And everywhere around us there is new life to be found.

He really is delighted with the job when it is done,
For He knows that He has managed to accomplish 'two-in-one'!
Then He removes His washing - so that the sun can shine,
For He's finished His spring cleaning - and both heaven and earth
look fine!

𝒴

Glenariff

Spring is returning once more to the Glen,
Wakened from sleep serene,
Paint me a picture of woodland and hills,
Colour it evergreen,
Quaint little town at the foot of the vale,
Sheltering 'neath the glen,
Capture its beauty, time cannot erase,
Ever it will remain.

Paint in the memories of bygone years,
Summertime's glory behold,
Colour the dark winding path with wild flowers,
Purple and crimson and gold,
Glenariff waterfall, touched by the sun,
Rose-coloured crystal hue,
Misty-clad mountains and streamlets at play,
Colour the heavens blue.

Colour Glenariff, and capture the scene,
Colour the Glens in all shades of green,
Colour Glenariff's beauty for me,
Colour the vision in my memory.

Evergreen valley is tinted with gold,
Autumn has sung her refrain,
Colour the changes that time will behold,
Re-create nature again,
Sheltering yonder, the woodland is still,
Colour the winter blue,
Capture Glenariff's rare beauty for me,
Memories forever renew.

The Lark Ascending

Rising upon a song
The lark ascends –
Borne upon a morning breeze -
He soars upwards towards the heavens,
Then circling the sky in animated flight,
Suddenly swoops downwards again
Towards the hills and valleys,
Playing with the sunlight
Filtering through the outspread branches of the trees,
He rests upon a bough as if listening to the earth,
Completely in tune with nature.
On the breath of the wind,
The lark once more ascends –
Soaring higher and higher -
Finding a vantage point
The performance begins -
Capturing his audience
He sings a melodious song of pure delight!
Wafting on the morning air,
Tremulous and beautiful,
Sensitive and sweet,
Finding notes of purity
Which the human voice can never reach!
Listening expectantly, as if waiting for the world's applause,
He gives an encore even more vibrant still -
Then, beguiling our hearts forever,
The lark takes one final bow,
Leaving the earth to entertain the heavens -
Drifting beyond the clouds -
Invisible -
Ascending on wings of song
To Infinity.

Listening to the Lark Ascending by the composer Vaughan Williams inspired this poem.

𝒴

Carrickfergus Castle

In the olde worlde town of Carrickfergus,
A Medieval Castle you will see,
On rugged crags she reigns in ancient glory,
Guarding Belfast Lough for centuries.

Towering above the fishing port so picturesque,
On land and sea she's given pride of place,
As Carrickfergus nestles in her shadow,
The Castle stands with dignity and grace.

Beside the sheltering hills of Carrickfergus,
St. Nicholas's Church comes into view,
At one in war and peace they've stood together,
To their people they've remained faithful and true.

Within her age-ed walls she holds the secrets,
Of battles fought and won so mightily,
By brave and gallant men who fought for Ulster,
Guarding this fortress with integrity.

The Castle's cornerstone remains untarnished,
Her Tower and her fortress still secure,
Though furrows of past times have left their traces,
She stands forever steadfast proud and sure.

This Anglo-Norman castle was built in the 12th century. Besieged in turn by Scots, Irish, English, and French. Taken by William III in 1690. The castle saw action right up until World War II. Standing by Belfast Lough in all her splendour reflecting 800 years of history.

Scenes of Antrim

The beauty of the Causeway coast is captured by this land,
Where Atlantic waves of ocean blue, embrace its golden
sands,
In rugged splendour gazing down the White Rocks are
arrayed,
Upon the 'strand of memories' where we as children played.

Follow along the winding road, a castle you will see,
Its age-ed charm is captured by Dunluce for centuries,
Port Ballintrae so picturesque we're privileged to view,
Then on to dear old Bushmills, where you'll drink a toast or
two.

Telling a legendary tale, Giant's Causeway wild and free,
The Isle of Rathlin, Fairhead's cliffs, such scenic majesty -
I'll take you to Port Braddan where a little church you'll find,
Nestling close to Whitepark Bay where sea and sand
entwine.

Turn down the road to Ballintoy where you can stay a while,
You'll see the rope bridge swaying as the salmon you
beguile,
Then picture Ballycastle and the Antrim Glens so fair,
With the beauty of the Causeway Coast nothing can
compare.

The Causeway Coast in Co. Antrim is renowned for its scenic beauty.

𝒴

Where Eagles Dare

High upon rocky mountain crags
The eagle reigns in majesty,
Proudly he watches his young,
Sheltering under their mother's wings,
Soft as eiderdown,
Safe and secure from all harm.
Leaving the nest he perches on the edge of the cliff,
Fixing his eye upon the blue awakening sea,
Waiting with eyes alert to capture his prey,
Ready to invade the ocean,
Planning his descent with split second precision,
And visual perception.
Suddenly he drops, talons ready to strike!
Cutting through the giant curling waves,
As the sea yields her wares to his grasp,
Succumbing to wildlife survival.
On powerful wings he reaches the mountain crags
Where mother and offspring feed.
Satisfied that all is well,
The eagle soars towards the heavens,
Lifting his wings of majesty,
Encircling the early morning sky,
In all its glory.
The sky darkens, storm clouds appear,
And lightning pervades the sky,
On wings of burnished gold he rides upon the storm,
Rivalling the elements,
Swerving and swooping back and forth
Taking freedom's flight.
Daring to mount upon Eagles wings
Towards the glorious light of eternity,
Paying homage to the Eternal Ruler of the world,
In all His splendour.
Suddenly the storm abates,
From parting clouds the eagle appears,
Encircling the sky once more,
He takes his leave of the heavens
And returns to his throne,
Where he reigns supreme.

Psalm 121

I lift up mine eyes and I behold the green and sheltering
hills,
And I know God watches over me as each promise He
fulfils,
For though my steps may falter, He will not let me fall,
And His right hand will guide me, when on His name I call.

His shadow will protect me from the sun that shines by day,
And the moon by night will light my path when I have lost
my way,
He has promised He will guard me from all evil and all
strife,
To the Maker of both heaven and earth, I will entrust my life.

And my eternal Father, enthroned in heaven above,
Will abide with me forever, so steadfast is His love,
As I gaze upon the sheltering hills, His promises He keeps,
For He is the God of Israel, and slumbers not, nor sleeps.

———————————— 𝒴 ————————————

The Sermon on the Mount

There were people of all ages
Gathered on the mountainside,
Poor and humble men and women,
"Bring the children too", He cried.
He was standing there before them,
And His heart was filled with love,
As He spoke to them and taught them
Words from Heaven above.

As they received His message
Telling people how to live,
And they gazed upon the Master
Showing people how to give.
Standing there with His disciples
Meek and lowly by His side,
They could see the 'Lamb of God',
And the 'Saviour' glorified.

As the glory of God's presence
Touched the people on that hill,
The 'Beatitudes of Jesus'
Are forever with us still.
And if you can show compassion
With a gentle, loving heart,
You will receive God's blessing,
And His love always impart.

The Beatitudes

The Saviour of the World is calling you,
To meet with Him upon the mountainside,
Reaching out to bless you with His love,
His everlasting arms are open wide.

The poor in spirit listen to His voice,
For in God's heavenly kingdom they belong,
To those who mourn He sends a comforter,
Healer of wounds, His mighty arms are strong.

The meek are blessed when at the Saviour's feet,
The earth's inheritance is theirs to claim,
The hungry and the thirsty soul He feeds,
Seeking righteousness in Jesus name.

The merciful seek mercy in His eyes,
And are rewarded by His look of love,
The pure in heart are humbled by His grace,
And see the face of God in heaven above.

The peacemakers find blessing at His side,
Children of God, so worthy of His name,
The righteous one the world will not molest,
While hope of Heaven's Kingdom still remains.

In faith come gather on the mountainside,
Those who have suffered much because of me,
And let your heart and soul rejoice and sing,
The greatness of the Lord one day you'll see.

Easter

Consider the Lilies

As the first pink blush of sunrise awakes the lily fair,
Her petals are unfolding under God's protecting care,
For there in sweet simplicity and beauty unadorned,
She blooms in all her glory, this flower that God has formed.

In wondrous colours she is clothed, reflecting earth and sky,
Her perfume leaves a fragrance as the gentle breeze drifts by,
In delicate profusion she grows beneath God's heaven,
Dependant on His providence which He has freely given.

But the 'Lily of the Valley' was born beneath the shade,
In the 'Garden of Gethsemane' were found her berries red,
With snow-white bells of purity and love God did adorn,
To greet the 'Risen Saviour' on that first Easter morn.

Beside the cool green pastures where the 'Water Lily' grows,
Her soft lips kiss the dewdrops as she dreams in quiet repose,
Considered by the heavens still more beautiful and fair,
Forever she will blossom, under God's eternal care.

Was it for Me?

Suffering and pain is etched
Upon your face of innocence -
And is it love I see?
Why have you been crucified upon a cross of shame?
Sinless and blameless, Lord was it for me?
Is it contrition's tears that flow from eyes that seldom weep?
As my cold heart cries out in penitence,
Lord in your heavenly kingdom will you please remember
me?
Your saving grace sufficient recompense.

Those out-stretched hands, though nail-pierced,
Have they still the power to heal?
With love so deep that it can touch my soul,
Could it be that you are listening to a dying sinner's plea?
Lord cleanse me by your blood and make me whole,
And now the light is fading and death is drawing near,
And shadows pass before my closing eyes,,
But in that dying moment I hear my Saviour's voice
"Today you'll dwell with me in paradise".

The dying thief's encounter with Jesus on Calvary's cross

𝓎

Calvary's Road

Up Calvary's Road I travelled,
Each step was fraught with care,
The burden that I carried
Seemed too much for me to bear!
I stopped for just a moment,
To ease my heavy load -
Then tenderly He lifted it from me
On Calvary's Road.

We walked along together,
And the Lord said "Do not fear",
"For every time you stumble,
You will find that I am here".
And when we came to Calvary,
He reached down lovingly,
And laid my burden at the cross
Where He had died for me.

Then through the mist of gratitude,
I suddenly could see,
Beyond the cross of suffering,
My Lord was beckoning me -
Then hand-in-hand together
Up Calvary's Hill we climbed,
And entered into Heaven
To find 'God's Love Divine'.

𝒴

The Greatest Love Story

Beside the Galilean Sea
The words He softly spoke to me,
Revealed the greatest love story,
This world has ever known.
The Holy Spirit, like a dove,
Came down and stilled the restless world,
I saw the Glory of the Lord,
At Galilee.

Upon the Cross of Calvary,
As my Lord and Saviour died for me,
He told the greatest love story,
This world has ever known,
The sky was dark, the air was still,
A hush came over Calvary's hill,
He paid love's sacrifice for me,
At Calvary.

He walked upon Lake Galilee,
He bore the cross to Calvary,
To tell the greatest love story,
This world has ever known.
His love is deeper than the sea,
The cross has conquered Calvary,
In Heaven we'll find His love story,
The greatest ever known.

Doubting Thomas

The disciples' hearts were sorrowful as they gathered there,
Mourning the death of Jesus crucified,
When suddenly the risen Lord appeared to them,
Showing his nail-pierced hands and wounded side.

"Peace be unto you" He said, - as they believed,
Filling their grieving hearts with hope and joy,
And then upon each soul the holy spirit breathed,
Giving them power which nothing could destroy.

But Thomas doubted it was Jesus who appeared to them,
Or if they'd spoken to the Son of God,
"Unless I touch his hands, and feel his pierced side,
I will not believe I've seen the risen Lord".

Again the Master stood within the midst of them,
"Thomas", He said, "behold my hands and side!"
"And be not faithless, but believe in me!"
"O Lord you are my God, the crucified".

"Because you've seen my nail prints you believe in me,
Blessed are those who believe, yet have not seen,"
For they have found the road to heaven, through Calvary,
Following where the living Christ has been.

The Love of Mary Magdalene

As Jesus Christ was crucified
Upon a cruel cross of shame,
A lonely figure watched him die
In agony and pain,
For it was Mary Magdalene,
Who had the precious spices poured
Upon the feet of Jesus,
Because she loved her Lord.

And as they nailed his hands and feet,
And placed the crown of thorns,
Calling him 'King of the Jews',
In mockery and scorn,
Mary wished that she could use
Those precious spices rare,
To heal the wounds of Jesus,
As she watched him dying there.

She brought the spices to the tomb,
Just before the break of day,
But when she came upon the sepulchre,
The stone was rolled away.
"Please tell me where they've laid my Lord?"
She asked the gardener,
'Mary, why do you weep'?
The voice of Jesus spoke to her.

And in the glory of that moment
She beheld her risen Lord,
As Jesus whispered 'Mary'
Her faith was then restored,
She returned to the disciples,
And her heart was full of joy,
For she had everlasting love
That nothing could destroy.

But deeper still was Jesus' love for Mary Magdalene,
And Mary knew that in heaven, His love would still remain.

Calvary to Heaven

Behold the Saviour of the world upon a rugged cross,
Offering his redeeming love and forgiveness to the lost,
For us he walked the lonely road of suffering and pain,
From Calvary to Heaven so that we might live again.

As the darkening shadows fell upon the hill of Calvary,
The sacrifice of Jesus was there for all to see,
Bearing the scars of sin upon his hands and wounded side,
There on the cruel cross of shame our Lord was crucified.

And when they laid his body in the tomb so dark and bare,
They did not know the Saviour of the world was lying there,
But when they visited the sepulchre early on Easter day,
They found that it was empty and the stone was rolled
away.

Then the glory of the risen Lord was revealed upon that
morn,
Soon to His Heavenly Father their Master would be gone,
For the world had found a Saviour, Heaven's doors were
open wide,
Because the Christ of Calvary for our transgressions died.

From Calvary to Heaven is the road we all must take,
To meet the risen Saviour, who suffered for our sake,
And there in Heaven's glory we'll see him face to face,
The spotless Lamb of Calvary who died to take our place.

No Greater Love

Sentenced to die in innocence on Calvary's cross,
Bearing the scorn and malice of the Jews,
Hatred's ears were deaf onto His anguished cry,
"Forgive them, for they know not what they do!"
The Saviour's dying prayer was all that Heaven required,
Whispered on fleeting breath to God above,
To save and bring salvation's hope to all mankind,
His life he gave – there was no greater love.

Sentenced to death by man's mistaken majesty,
Whose aspirations likened unto God!
He died in order to fulfil His destiny,
Bearing the condemnation of the world.
Mingling with the crimson blood of Calvary,
Nothing but love could melt those hearts of stone,
Conquering death, there was no greater love than this!
God's Sacrificial Lamb our sins atoned.

And still we mock and scorn the Christ of Calvary,
Though some 2,000 years have been and gone,
In all our self-sufficiency we still ignore,
Redemption's cross which Jesus died upon.
Because love's sacrifice has triumphed over sin,
He'll hear your fleeting whisper of a prayer,
Come to the Christ of Calvary, there is no greater love,
Salvation from the Lord awaits your there.

The Answer

What is the answer to my Life Lord?
Somehow I thought I had it all -
Wanting more and more of this world's pleasures,
Never heeding poverty's warning call.

In depths of pain and degradation,
Losing life's grip upon reality!
My troubled soul is searching for an answer -
Lord can you save a sinner such as me?

Beneath the rock of ages you'll find refuge,
My sheltering love will guard you come what may,
And by God's saving grace you'll find the answer,
When the world from you has turned away.

At the foot of Calvary's Cross I'll lift your burdens,
Together we will walk from day to day,
I will be there to strengthen and sustain you,
When you feel alone upon life's way.

Reaching down and lifting up the fallen,
Walking once again on higher ground,
When on the mighty rock of God you're standing,
The answer to your life you will have found.

Beneath the rock of ages you'll find refuge,
His sheltering love will guard you come what may,
And by God's saving grace you'll find the answer,
When the world from you has turned away.

Y

I Will Never Leave
the Heart That Loves Me

I come into your presence Lord in reverence,
Seeking to find God's strength which you impart,
Trusting in the Christ of Calvary,
I offer unto you a loving heart.

A heart of love my child is all I ask of you,
The greatest gift in life you have to give,
Abide in me as I abide in you my child,
Come unto me in Jesus' name and live.

For I will never leave the heart that loves me,
Forever I am yours and you are mine,
Within my loving arms let me enfold you,
In my embrace you'll find God's love divine.

Communion
Luke 22 V.15

Beloved one I earnestly desire
To share with you the Passover Divine,
Come follow me into the Upper Room,
And from my hands receive the bread and wine.

Partake with Peter from redemption's cup,
And let denial's tears your sin erase,
Where Judas sat, the Lord is beckoning you,
To find contrition in betrayal's place.

I enter now into the Upper Room,
And in your presence Lord I take my place,
Humbly I feed upon the bread of life,
And drink salvation's cup of saving grace.

Jesus my Lord, redeeming love is mine,
Guide and protect and keep me from all harm,
Cleansed from my sin forever I will be,
Held in my Saviour's Everlasting Arms.

Y

Summer

Summer Midnight

Moonglow, starlight and mystical sky,
At midnight caress as the clouds drift by,
Silver reflection shining through,
Diamonds of heaven's crystal hue.

Moonglow and starlight's radiant smile,
Brightens the world for just a while,
Night shades of heaven, silver and gold,
Wonderful moment of glory behold.

Shadowy clouds obscure the moon,
The vanishing stars disappear too soon,
Forever the scene is gone from sight,
Only memories remain of this magical night.

Y

The Sunflower

In the darkness of night she slept,
As the shadowy clouds crept by,
Her colours of golden hue,
Unseen by the human eye.
But God in heaven above,
Enfolded her in his care,
Keeping her safe from harm,
This delicate flower so fair.

At the first light of dawn she arose,
A sunflower in beauty arrayed,
To drink in the morning dew,
She lifted her beautiful head.
Her petals of purest gold,
Rivalled the morning sun,
As she swayed on the gentle breeze,
Another day had begun.

But time is a precious thing,
And soon it will slip away,
Her petals of purest gold,
Will wither and then decay.
But God in heaven above,
Will enfold her in his care,
And in His time she will return,
More glorious and fair.

Evergreen

You look so wild and beautiful in your entirety,
For you are God's own masterpiece created in a tree.
Your leaves grow in abundance as they bedeck your hair,
And Mother Nature weaves the gown you elegantly wear.

Your heart is strong and faithful, though tender are your
charms,
For you will fondly cradle the songbirds in your arms,
As they nestle in your bosom, you rock them to and fro,
Providing rest and shelter from the stormy winds that blow.

You are a 'special mother', the wild flowers would agree,
As they spray their scented perfume upon your shawl of
green,
And weave for you a garland to tie around your gown,
For they know you will 'forget-them-not' as your leafy head
looks down.

The little woodland creatures by some are seen to play
Under your pale green petticoat to pass the time away,
As you keep nature's secrets so safely hidden there,
They have no need to worry when they are in your care.

This world can never measure God's great affinity
With the miracles of nature in the creation of a tree,
But every creature great and small upon this earthly scene,
Is dependant on God's providence, for His love is
'Evergreen'.

𝒴

The Rose

Peeping out from the shadows, blushing alone,
Grows the 'rose of compassion' in my childhood home,
Her sweet scented fragrance, silken petals did bear,
As she once bloomed profusely in this garden fair,
Tended and nurtured by my father's hand,
With care and with pleasure so lovingly planned.

As I tenderly touch your petals so fair,
I think of the gardener no longer there,
Now the weeds of destruction have left you bereft,
And one single blossom is all that is left,
As a tear of remembrance falls from my eye,
Nostalgia lingers from days long gone by.

So live on fairest rose in my childhood home,
Peeping out from the shadows, blushing alone,
Sweet reminiscence of halcyon days,
When in my father's garden we laughed and we played,
May you bloom forever as your petals unfold,
For you've left me with memories more precious than gold.

Down by the Watermill

As we walked beside the river, down by the watermill,
The first time we were together, the forgotten world stood
still,
Our springtime love we vowed forever, beside the daffodils,
Memories of our love still linger, down by the watermill.

As we picked the perfumed bluebells, wandering through
the glen,
In our hearts our springtime love would always return
again,
Arms entwined around each other, seems many years since
then,
Memories of our love still linger, wandering through the
glen.

Waterwheel turn around and around -
Listen, you'll hear the murmuring sound,
Turn on and on where lovers meet,
Down by the watermill.

Here is the glen, come see the river, here is the watermill,
Come find the path where we walked together, our dreams
we remember still,
With passing years our love's grown deeper, and our vows
we have fulfilled,
Memories of our love still linger, down by the watermill.

Waterwheel turn around and around -
Listen, you'll hear the murmuring sound,
Turn on and on where lovers meet,
Down by the watermill.

———————————— *Y* ————————————

Autumn

Autumn Unawares

In smiling subtlety she has appeared,
With golden vein her trellised patterns trace,
The falling leaves succumb to nature's touch,
And suddenly she's stolen summer's place!

Once outspread branches sprinkled with the dew,
Were clothed in summer's favourite shades of green,
But now in amber colours they are dressed,
And lie where floral blossoms once were seen.

In nature's guise came autumn unawares,
Yielding her harvest gems of burnished gold,
More beautiful the first sunlight of dawn,
When summer wakes her glories to unfold.

Harvest

We celebrate the harvest, bringing gifts of love,
Flowers and fruit and vegetables, sent from heaven above,
Sheaves of wheat and loaves of bread, heads of golden corn,
Welcome the harvest season as they the church adorn.

Harvest shades of orange, yellow, green and gold,
Flowers in every colour of Autumn we behold,
Choral voices singing, all with one accord,
Lift their hearts in thankfulness and joy onto the Lord.

Rustic leaves are falling, shimmering in the sun,
Harvest time is over, winter has begun,
But seedtime and harvest will return again,
And this golden season forever will remain.

The Power of Nature

The Power of Nature

The darkest night succumbs to the power of nature,
And from depths of her soul
The silver moon shines through the darkness,
Filtering through the clouds and chasing the shadows.

The night draws to a close,
As the moon drifts beyond the horizon,
The sun rises -
By light's revelation the earth awakens.

Surrounded by morning's glory
All nature greets the new day,
My spirit ascends,
Leaving behind the terrors of night.

Touched by heaven's healing balm,
Mind and soul renewed,
My heart fills with hope and joy,
And I behold the glory of God.

Braving the Storm

Shadowed is the night,
The moon's eerie reflection fades into obscurity,
As ghost-like clouds pervade the sky,
From turbulent storm-tossed waters,
Giant waves rear up to meet the heavens,
Midnight blue and sea green mingling together,
Tossed to and fro by the wind from height to depth.
In spectacular motion,
Indescribable chaos erupts with a vengeance,
The sea plunges with mighty force,
Venting her anger against the rocks,
Leaving destruction in her wake.

Reflected in the eye of the storm,
A pale light flickers from a fisherman's lamp,
His boat left to devices beyond his control,
Her anchor battling against the ferocious elements
Threatening to overcome the vessel.
The waves rise higher and higher -
Fighting to keep afloat
Amidst the turbulent waters,
Rebuked by the relentless ocean,
Driven nearer and nearer to the rocks,
Succumbing to the cruel forces,
The fishing boat tosses in helpless abandonment.

Suddenly, the turmoil of the night passes,
The sun in her ascendancy appears on the horizon,
Taken unawares the sky changes from grey to blue,
Water colours filter through the clouds.
Racing in blurred motion,
The sea turns towards the morning light,
The storm subsides.
Instantly calm emerges from the deep,
Chaos forgotten,
In visionary beauty the ocean gently flows,
On the crest of the waves,
The fishing boat glides safely home.

Galilean Memories

Beyond the storms and turmoil of the busy world,
I hear the voice of Jesus calling me,
Forget your cares and worries, leave them all behind,
Meet me by the Galilean sea.

Let me calm the ocean of your troubled heart,
Follow me as in the days of yore,
Put your hand into your heavenly Father's hand,
The hand that stilled the waves upon the shore.

Then silently a blessed peace steals o'er my heart,
As the wonder of the ocean speaks to me,
The sunlight's golden rays light up the morning sky,
Shining upon the Galilean sea.

And suddenly the busy world seems far away,
As Jesus walks beside me on the shore,
The storms of life are in my heavenly Father's hands,
And I will trust in Him forever more.

--------------------- *Y* ---------------------

Winter

Silent Worship

Winter is lost in silent reverie,
As the first snowdrop's silver frosted petals,
So fragile and beautiful,
Melt like jewelled teardrops.
Gently warmed by the whispering breath of spring,
The crickets and bees with trembling wings,
Embrace a world of unfolding beauty,
Drinking from the freshly showered daffodils.
Seduced by the sweet scented lilacs,
The blackbird sings in early expectancy,
Her song unrivalled by nature.
Suddenly the earth is infused
With wondrous colours of delicate perfection,
Touched by Creation's hand
The world looks on in silent worship,
And God is in His heaven.

Sky Scenes

Soft mountain snow clouds, shadowy peaks,
In rippling wavelets infinity speaks,
Vastness immeasurable, celestial blue,
Oceanic reflections in heaven we view.

Moment by moment life-changing scenes,
Sun-filtering artistry's vision supreme,
Divine intervention by heaven's fair hand,
Ethereal beauty unspoiled by man.

Mystical images float in the air,
Capture the eye on a wing and a prayer,
Watching as nature unveils the scene,
Unique revelation, perfection serene.

Intriguing mastery for all to see,
Heaven and earth in sublime harmony,
Immortal infusion of colours so rare,
In glorious beauty, beyond compare.

Wonders of Winter

Silver-topped mountains,
Pale morning sunshine,
Icicle Rainbows,
Pearl drops falling free.
Red-breasted Robin,
Cry of a seagull,
White -feathered snow shower,
Winter-blue sea.

Vast world of beauty,
White shimmering satin,
Covering earth's secrets
That no-one can learn.
Frost-crusted snowflakes
Make intricate patterns,
Fall for one moment,
And never return.

Voices of children,
Wafting on clear air,
Winter-bright colours,
Red, green and blue.
Focus the scene,
And capture the memory,
This wonderful Season
Will vanish too soon.

November Magic

Magical November evening,
How beautiful is your sky,
In borrowed colours of summer,
The sun-tinted clouds float by.
And like a stained-glass window,
As the sun begins to set,
The most wonderful colours of nature,
Like a rainbow silhouette -
In red and gold and crimson,
Edged with turquoise and peach,
Appear upon the horizon,
So near, yet just out of reach.
And in that parting moment,
As daylight slips away,
The magic colours of summer
New beauty will display,
Then the moonlight greets the sunset,
As the stars light up the sky,
The magical November evening
Kisses the world goodbye.

Christmas

God's Miracle Divine

Along the road they travelled, as from Nazareth they came,
Just a little farther, and they'd reach Bethlehem,
The inn-keeper was unconcerned as he saw Mary's plight,
He did not know the Son of God would be born upon that night.

He offered them a stable, so cold, so dark, so bare,
And Mary bore God's only Son within the manger there,
Then suddenly a glorious star lit up the meagre place,
And The Glory of the Lord shone down upon the baby's face.

With a heart so full of thankfulness she held her little one,
For she had been God's Chosen One to bear His only son!
There in Bethlehem's manger, she'd fulfilled God's Heavenly plan,
And brought His child into the world to be the Son of Man!

For a few more hours she'd hold him, her precious baby son, -
Then she would share him with the world, upon that Christmas morn,
For Mary knew within her heart that God's Miracle Divine,
Born that night at Bethlehem, was the Saviour of Mankind.

Christmas Glory

Arrayed in Christmas glory heaven reached down to earth,
And earth was raised to infinite heights sublime,
Beyond human comprehension Christ was born into the
world,
God's spiritual gift of love divine.
The wonder of God's miracle was to the world revealed,
As the infant babe was born upon that night,
And love came down at Christmas as Mary held her child,
Transforming this world's darkness into light.

Arrayed in Christmas glory heaven still reaches to this
world,
And lifts our souls to infinite heights above,
Offering us salvation through God's redeeming grace,
Enfolding us in everlasting love,
Although 2,000 years have passed the world still celebrates,
The miracle of Jesus' lowly birth,
For there we found communion with our Lord upon the
night,
When in Christmas glory heaven came down to earth.

From Bethlehem to Calvary

The earth is clothed in purity and innocence,
As silently the heavenly snow appears,
Creation's Christmas Glory wrapped in swaddling clothes,
Greets Bethlehem's Saviour for 2,000 years.

In Heaven's eternal glow the night is sleeping,
As countless stars the midnight sky adorn,
Upon the world their watchful vigil keeping,
The firmament proclaiming Christ is born.

But unawares another year is stealing,
The heavenly snow has vanished all too soon,
And Calvary's scarlet cloak is now appearing,
As shadows of the earth eclipse the moon.

Because Christ's crimson stains of crucifixion,
Covered this darkened earth so long ago,
Creation, clothed in resurrection's glory,
Wears Christmas swaddling clothes as white as snow.

*In the year 2000 the snow fell pure and white, reminding us of the true
meaning of Christmas.*
*On 9th January, 2001, we had a total eclipse of the moon. The sky turned dark
and then red reminding us of Christ's Crucifixion*

God's Message in the Snow

Where was the Christ of Christmas in 1995?
With money spent on presents the Belfast shops did thrive,
In the midst of all the hustle and the bustle of the mob,
So few of us remembered about the Son of God.

Some went to church to worship upon that Christmas Eve,
And still the shops were open, more money to receive,
Then came the preparations for the following Christmas day,
Somehow the Christ of Christmas seemed very far away.

But then - so unexpectedly - came the softly falling snow,
Clothing the earth in purity and holiness below,
No costly gift or present with its beauty could compare,
And in the stillness of the night the Son of God was there.

A blessed peace descended upon the earth so pure and
white,
As the Lord revealed His 'Message in the Snow' upon that
night,
For 'purity' and 'holiness' are gifts we cannot buy,
But Christ was there at Christmas, as the snow fell from the
sky.

The Promise of Salvation

In the stillness of the holy night the world was unaware,
That the promise of salvation lay within a stable bare,
And looking down from heaven God beheld His baby son,
Knowing that on this Christmas night His purpose had begun.

The shepherds watched in wonderment as the star revealed Christ's birth,
And the wise men travelled from the east with gifts of greatest worth,
The angels sang a glorious song to greet the infant child,
And Mary looked upon his face, so gentle, meek and mild.

She held her precious baby with a heart so full of love,
His outstretched hands would bring God's gift of healing from above,
For Jesus came to heal the sick, the blind, the halt, the lame,
And reconcile the world to God in His Heavenly Father's name.

But this little child of Bethlehem would be spat upon and scorned,
And the head that Mary cradled would wear a crown of thorns,
Those outstretched hands, so perfect, would be nailed upon a cross,
And Christ would die in agony and pay salvation's cost.

Over two thousand years have passed and Christmas comes again,
Christ's lowly birth is only remembered now and then,
Of the true miracle of Christmas the world still seems unaware,
But those who come to worship Him will find heaven waiting there.

God's Heavenly Miracle

Arrayed in Christmas glory heaven reached down to earth,
And earth was raised to infinite heights sublime,
As love came down at Christmas clothed in childlike
innocence,
God's spiritual gift of Love Divine.

The guiding star of Bethlehem shone down on that night,
Upon the scene of Christ's nativity,
Worshipping Christ the Saviour within the manger stall,
Wise men and shepherds knelt in humility.

And with unchanging faithfulness, God reaches down to
earth,
And lifts our souls to infinite heights sublime,
Lightening our darkness with life-transforming power,
In Christ re-born by infinite Love Divine.

New Year

The Circle of Life

Looking back on the year that's departed,
As life's circle spins slowly around,
Some people found peace and contentment,
And for some their world turned upside down,
But God holds our lives in the balance,
And he will not let us fall,
And the circle of life is still turning,
For He is the Lord over all.

For some the new year will bring blessing,
And for others, fortune and fame,
But closer to God than breathing,
Are those who bear sorrow and pain,
For He will give strength and courage,
If on Him alone we depend,
For the circle of life is unbroken,
And His love it will never end.

As we move on from season to season,
In this new year that God has given,
Let us put our trust in the Master,
Who is Lord of earth and heaven,
Let Him join His hand with your hand,
In the circle of His love,
And walk with Him into the future,
Trusting in God above.

Millennium Worship

In those first life-defining moments,
As we celebrate the New Millennium,
Lift up your eyes,
Behold the galaxy!
Nothing on earth will ever compare,
With heaven's infinity.

In those first life-defining moments,
As we celebrate the New Millennium,
Acknowledge God's creation,
And His vast eternal plan,
Remember He holds the Universe,
In the hollow of His hand.

In those first life-defining moments,
As we celebrate the New Millennium,
His name shall be called Jesus,
Saviour and Lord of all,
His image is not found in the Millenium Dome -
But in Bethlehem's manger stall.

In those first life-defining moments,
As we celebrate the New Millennium,
Fall on your knees
And worship the Prince of Peace,
For He is the Lord of heaven and earth,
And His kingdom will never cease.

Y

The New Jerusalem

Zion's River

From heaven's eternal city,
A crystal river flows,
And from its source, life giving power,
Upon the world bestows.

The tree of life is standing,
Its healing branches bear
God's living fruit, those who partake,
Eternal life will share.

And through the streets of Zion,
God's healing river flows,
With water of everlasting life,
Heaven's blessing is disclosed.

The Holy City's righteousness,
Shines forth like the dawn,
Source of all life and truth and power,
Jerusalem reborn.

Come drink from Zion's river,
And glorify His name,
The Lamb who sits upon the throne,
Reigns in Jerusalem.

The New Jerusalem

I dream of the New Jerusalem,
So beautiful and fair,
Unveiled by resurrection light,
Like precious jewels rare.
A crystal river flowing,
With mercy love and grace,
The face of God I will behold,
Within that holy place.

I dream of the New Jerusalem,
So beautiful and fair,
The morning star in glory shines,
Upon the temple there.
The blest will live forever,
And know no grief or pain,
And in the dwelling place of God,
Forever will remain.

Music

Music

Music is the inspiration of the soul,

The sensation of touch,

Responsive fingers

Moving upon an instrument

With deepest sensitivity.

The vibrating heart

In harmonic communion with the soul,

Creating a melody of intricate beauty,

Beyond all comprehension,

A meditation upon a theme,

A heavenly crescendo that never dies,

A diminuendo of utmost tranquillity,

Lingering in the memory

Forever.

Upon Piano Keys

There is a place within God's House,
Reserved especially for me,
Where I communicate with Him,
Upon piano keys.

I dedicate this gift to God,
As in His presence prayerfully,
I play each song of thanks to Him,
Upon piano keys.

As soul to soul we play our part,
Attune with God in harmony,
In reverence I worship Him,
Upon piano keys.

The music rises like a prayer,
Embracing every melody,
A sacrifice of praise to Him,
Upon piano keys.

The gifts of God are wonderful,
But the most precious gift to me,
Is the music of the Master played,
Upon piano keys.

The Music Man's Song

He entertains the Belfast folk as they walk to and fro,
As he sings all different kinds of songs, some quick, and others slow.
And if by chance you happen to give him a coin or two,
He will be very happy to bid good-day to you.

So many times I've seen this Music Man in the arcade,
And heard a favourite melody upon his guitar played.
He always looks so happy as he smiles at passers by,
And he makes Belfast a brighter place - this no-one can deny.

Well just as I was walking through the town the other day,
There came the sound of music from the arcade just down the way.
I paused for just a moment! - I could hear a sacred song!
And the voice which sang the chorus to this man did belong.

He sang - "Be still for the presence of the Lord, the Holy One is here,
Come bow before Him now, in reverence and fear,
In Him no sin is found - we stand on holy ground,
Be still for the presence of the Lord, the Holy One is here."

The message was so moving, as he sang quietly there,
And to me his words brought comfort and peace beyond compare.
And as I stopped to talk to him I discovered he belonged
To a Christian Church renewal group, where he praised the Lord in song.

So if by chance your passing and you hear this 'Music Man',
Perhaps you'll take the time to think and wonder at God's plan!
In this world his riches may be few - yet he has everything!
For somehow I think in God's eyes, this Music Man is a king!

This man played in Belfast every Saturday and brought blessing to many people.

———————————— 𝒴 ————————————

Midnight Nocturne

As the descending shadows,
O'er the horizon creep,
Strains of a midnight nocturne,
Caress my soul in sleep,
Music of quiet serenity,
Drifts on the balmy air,
Soothing my slumbering senses,
Like a nocturnal prayer.

On wings of inspiration,
The purple clouds steal by,
Nocturnal meditation,
Enchants the midnight sky,
Soft reverie of mystery,
Lulling my soul to sleep,
Stay with me till the dawning,
Your slumber song repeat.

Strains of nocturnal music,
Linger as I awake,
Gone on the breath of morning,
Will not my soul forsake,
Wondrous night of rapture,
Departing with the dawn,
Return again at midnight,
Immortal theme live on.

Y

Song without Words

There's a melody lingering within my mind,
A song without words which I cannot find,
Lord take this song and the music I feel,
Give me beautiful words, only you can reveal.

This song without words is so special to me,
The melody's there at the touch of a key,
But I need the words only you can impart,
Bringing glory to Jesus, and joy to my heart.

May the melody played and the words which you speak.
Bring a beautiful song to the people we meet.
May your words touch each soul, as the song lingers there,
Bringing your love and blessing beyond compare.

Lonesome Melody

Hear him strumming to the busy beat of life,
Homeless figure in a doorway,
Plays a melody recalled from bygone days,
Years of loneliness his story,
Who is he standing there? fighting cold and despair!
Doesn't anybody care?

Cold wind whistles to his 'Lonesome Melody',
Takes the rhythm from his fingers,
Through the years he's lost his friends and family,
But his hope in life still lingers,
Who is he standing there? fighting cold and despair!
Doesn't anybody care?

Oh won't you bring a smile to those sad and lonesome eyes?
Playing in his disguise, won't you show him that God cares?

Drop a coin down on the other side of life conveniently
forgotten,
Take a look - it could be you that's standing there, lost and
lonely and forsaken!
Who is he standing there? fighting cold and despair!
Why doesn't anybody care?

People walking on the other side of life, can you hear my
melody?
Lonesome Melody!

In Touch With God

You sing to me a love song which no-one else can hear,
For you are the God of heaven and your voice is ever near,
You play to me a melody only I can comprehend,
Together we're in harmony, my master and my friend.

You give me inspiration as I hear your voice divine,
In heavenly words of poetry our hearts and minds combine,
For the words that you have written from within your heart
of love,
Bring a spiritual blessing to my soul from heaven above.

You speak to me through nature in so many ways,
The wonder of this living world your handiwork displays,
Millions of heavenly miracles through your eyes I can see,
I thank you my creator for everything you share with me.

A Blessing In Song

from Ballyclare Male Choir

In the stillness of that lovely Sabbath evening,
The people came to church from near and far.
And in the House of God they joined together,
To listen to the singing of a choir.

I looked around and watched the congregation,
As the sound of choral singing filled the air,
For all their cares and sorrows were forgotten,
As God touched the hearts of every person there.

In joyful harmony they joined together,
In reverence as they sang a prayer to God,
And the cross of Jesus Christ reached out behind them,
As they lifted up their voices to the Lord.

And Jesus took the hands of the conductor,
As he stood beneath the shadow of the cross,
And to him He gave His blessed inspiration,
As the choral music conquered pain and loss.

Within the church upon that Sabbath evening,
The 'peace of God' descended like a dove,
As the voices of the choir all joined together,
Singing a prayer to God in heaven above.

If only we will pray to God our Father,
And live our earthly lives in harmony,
His hands, just like the hands of the conductor,
Will guide our lives through all eternity.

—————————— ℐ ——————————

Waterfall Music

Flow river flow on the voice of the wind,
Down the craggy mountain side,
Waterfall music and thunderous applause
Is echoing far and wide,
In spectacular beauty your presence we feel,
Like a pure and refreshing shower,
To the wonder of nature waterfall flow,
With majestic beauty and power.

Waterfall flow with a rhythmic pulse,
Vibrant and strong and free,
Wending your way to the valley below,
In a vision of purity,
Flow on and on where the river bends,
Meandering down to the sea,
There on the shore where the waters meet,
Follow your destiny.

Flow river flow where the distant voice
Of the ocean is calling to you,
Listen you'll hear the beckoning waves,
Sigh from the depths of blue,
Flow river flow to their welcoming arms,
For a moment we have to part,
But in Waterfall Music and thunderous applause,
I can still hear the beat of your heart.

A Glimpse of God

O Lord I do not really understand
The' spiritual meaning' of your plan,
Sometimes I find it difficult to see,
The truth contained within your word for me.
If I could only pray as others pray,
And know within my heart just what to say,
Then I would find your Holy Spirit there,
As I speak my faltering words to you in prayer.

But I have listened to a symphony,
A miracle created from a melody,
Or a concerto played upon a violin,
With delicacy touching every string.
And there I find the wondrous mind of God,
Behind each note so sensitively played,
A 'Masterpiece' created specially,
Inspired by God in perfect harmony.

Within my heart you've given unto me,
A love of music and of harmony,
Help me to be able to impart
The spiritual feelings of my heart,
And may I never underestimate
The beauty of the sounds which you create,
In an intricately woven melody,
As your orchestra performs a symphony.

y

Children's Poems

New-Born Love

My new-born child so beautiful, to you I've given birth,
And they were labour pains of love which brought you to
this earth,
Your outstretched hands are very small, but they are safe in
mine,
And I will never let them go, until the end of time.

I'll keep you for a little while, protected from all harm,
And lovingly I'll hold you, safe within my arms,
But as you grow and your young life will new direction take,
My heart will still be with you, for this bond you cannot
break.

I wish that I could always stay forever by your side,
But whatever may befall you, my arms are open wide,
To comfort and to strengthen you, and heal your hurt and
pain,
And when you falter on life's way, I'll lift you up again.

My new-born child so beautiful, whatever you become,
I dedicate your life to God, my precious little one,
May He safely keep you from harm along life's way,
May He guide your footsteps, for this I humbly pray.

And when one day I leave you for just a little while,
I'll still be watching over you, and protecting you my child,
And I'll still hold those baby hands, which once you placed
in mine,
And I will never let them go, until the end of time.

To celebrate the birth of my little grandson, Jack.

𝒴

The Gift of a Child
(Christening)

Little child so precious,
As I hold you in my arms,
May holy angels guard you,
And keep you from all harm.

We come into God's presence,
Upon this Christening Day,
For the blessing of our new born child,
Thank you Lord we pray.

As the sacred oil of blessing,
In baptism is poured,
May you always be forever,
In angel arms adored.

As Mother Mary wrapped
The Jesus Child in swaddling clothes,
May the love of God enfold you,
As heavenly blessings He bestows.

Little child so precious,
As you journey on life's way,
May God always walk before you,
And guide your footsteps come what may.

Do You Believe in Angels?

My little child with eyes like stars and golden flowing hair,
Lifts her voice to Heaven as she says a simple prayer,
"Do you believe in angels Mum? " she asks expectantly,
"A little angel unawares is exactly what I see."

Every time you say your prayers God's angels are about,
Filling you with goodness from the inside out,
Seeing the look of innocence upon your upturned face,
Angel's arms caress you with beauty and with grace.

And I believe God's angels float on wings of love,
Lighting up your little heart with sunshine from above,
Guarding and protecting you when you are at play,
Reaching down to touch you when you kneel to pray.

My little fair haired darling now you are asleep,
God's ministering angels will their heavenly vigil keep,
I lift my voice to heaven and say a simple prayer,
"Thank you Lord for sending my 'little angel unawares'."

Cara - little angel unawares

A Daisy for Mum

As sun-kissed daisies sway in the wind,
Each head so white and pure,
One flower is plucked and held with love,
In the hands of a wee boy of four.

"Here is a tiny daisy mum,
I'm giving this to you,
Don't you think it is very beautiful?
With petals as soft as dew."

"Can't you see its bright little yellow heart
Is the colour of the sun?"
Like the wonder beheld in a little boy's eyes,
As he gives the wild flower to his mum.

So gentle the touch of a little child,
So perceptive for one so young,
He is but a flower in the springtime of life,
When all is said and done.

The blossoms of love and gentleness,
Need nurtured like a flower,
Watered with drops of kindness,
Like a cool and refreshing shower.

I will never forget this moment,
Or the sweet little daisy fair,
Placed in my hand by my little son,
And held for a lifetime there.

Jack's Treasure

Cradle Love

She rocks the cradle gently as she sings a lullaby,
And as the gas light flickers, a tear falls from her eye,
Of her beloved husband only memories remain,
But in innocence her baby sleeps, and life begins again.

She rocks the cradle gently as she sings a lullaby,
Warming her work-worn fingers where the dying embers lie,
But there's a new tomorrow as night's shadows close around,
From within her heart of loneliness, a mother's love is found.

She rocks the cradle gently as she sings a lullaby,
Lighting a penny candle to happier times gone by,
But a brand new day is dawning in early morning grace,
As she looks upon her baby son, she sees his father's face.

She rocks the cradle gently as she sings a lullaby,
And through the filtering sunlight a smile lights up her eye,
And then in sweet remembrance she holds him to her breast,
And in that precious moment – the cradle is at rest.

My grandmother was left a widow very young. Her fourth child was just a little baby when
her husband died and she had to raise her family in very poor circumstances.

How Much Does Love Cost?

I look down from Heaven at my children born,
Into poverty, famine and war,
Their lives have no value, worth nothing at all,
And they can't understand what it's for,
I look into eyes of stark hunger and pain,
From a world where all hope is lost,
With nothing to live for, and no-one to care –
I wonder how much does love cost?

And I look through my tears at my children born
On the fortunate side of life,
Where they want for nothing that money can buy,
And still there is fighting and strife,
I find hatred and greed, and selfishness there,
But oh what a price has been paid!
In turning deaf ears to poverty's cries,
And living for self instead.

Can you give some help to a little child
Who has lost the reason to live?
My people are desperate for one crust of bread -
Can you find something to give?
Every heart-felt gift I will multiply,
And repay it, whatever the cost,
To wipe all the tears from my children's eyes
And bring hope to a world that is lost.

To wipe all the tears from my children's eyes?
I wonder how much does love cost?

Y

Mr. Wonderful!

The man in my life realised from the start,
With a look from his eyes he commanded my heart,
He can love me, can leave me, can make me feel blue,
But he knows, come what may, I will always be true.

I must fetch, I must carry, I must bend to his will,
And all of the time I keep saying "I will",
But the trust in his eyes and the love he can give,
Have captured my life for as long as I live.

He can laugh, he can frown and he'll boss when he can,
But my heart still belongs to this wonderful man,
Ah! my heart is all 'tied up' and I'll never be free,
For the man in my life is 'a wee boy of three'.

*This little poem was written by my Mother about my youngest child
Alan who was born just after my father died in 1980*

The Greatest Gift

A mother's love is the greatest gift that life bestows upon,
Her baby child so precious from the moment it is born,
Asking that God will bless this little one within her care,
Knowing in her arms she holds the answer to her prayers.

Guiding and protecting throughout childhood years,
Sharing, caring, comforting, with love dispelling fears,
Every precious moment with her children spent,
Knowing that the blessing of a child is heaven sent.

Giving instead of taking, asking for no reward,
Knowing when to let go and leave it to the Lord,
Watching as her children will new direction take,
Knowing that a mother's love is a bond that cannot break.

This love will last a lifetime, a priceless jewel rare,
That nothing separates and nothing can compare,
Her arms are always open, whatever may befall,
The blessing of a mother's love is the greatest gift of all.

Heaven's Embrace

I look upon my precious baby child,
Safe in my arms and held in heaven's embrace,
The early morn with grace and beauty smiles,
As eyes of love look down upon her face.

Her tiny heart beat throbbing close to mine,
God's wondrous gift, bestowed upon this day,
New life, creation's miracle divine,
Thank you for this child O Lord I pray.

My baby girl I place into your hands,
Her hopes, her dreams, whatever is to be,
As peacefully she sleeps within my arms,
Let Heaven's Embrace always begin with me.

To celebrate the birth of my little grand-daughter Cara Dawn.

y

Mischief Maker

Good morning 'mischief maker' with those big angel eyes,
And a look of perfect innocence which you cannot disguise,
A smile lights up your little face, perhaps you will be good,
But I can tell immediately, you don't really think you should,
For after all in baby world there's so much to explore,
And you will not be put off another a minute more.

And now I see you looking down your tiny turned up nose,
Wondering just what you can get up to I suppose,
You open wide your dimpled arms as I lift you from your cot,
And I smother you with kisses for I love you such a lot,
When placed upon your changing mat you give a little blink,
Discovering ten tiny toes so very clean and pink.

You laugh and squeal and giggle and think I'm very funny,
Then kicking frantically you twist and turn onto your tummy,
And now you are becoming just a little bored,
So in order to make very sure that you are not ignored,
You decide that you will give a yell and then pretend to cry,
Leaving it to mummy to work out the reason why.

Upon your baby face I see an unexpected frown,
And from your angel eyes two tiny tears come trickling down,
Then all at once they vanish and you smile from ear to ear,
And then as if by magic all your troubles disappear,
You've had enough of mummy so you want down and away,
Crawling on your hands and knees hide and seek to play.

On little wobbly legs you stand and then begin to toddle,
Wiggling your bottom to and fro just to show that it's a doddle,
In your tiny world of wonders there is so much to see,
And every single moment you want to play with me!
Sweet little 'mischief maker' your full of fun, no doubt,
My heart and soul you've captured and turned them inside-out.

This poem was written when my little grandson Jack was just beginning to walk.

Childhood Memories

Turn back the tide to my childhood days
Of make-believe and dreams,
Where we played by my Grandmother's village home,
T'was but yesterday it seems,
Bring back those moments of happiness,
Those memories dear to me,
Where as children we played by the shingle tide,
In our 'magic world' by the sea.

Those were the days of sweet innocence,
That I thought would last forever,
As we followed the path through the leafy glen,
And skipped by the banks of the river,
Go back in time to those summer days,
When we picked the wild meadow flowers,
And gathered the purple Iris's -
I remember those happy hours.

But we cannot return to our childhood days,
Nor we cannot turn back the tide,
And gone is the meadow where we used to play,
And the wild flowers are cast aside,
And gone is that dear little village home,
And our make-believe dreams by the sea,
But the ocean of time will never erase
Those days from my memory.

Heaven

Mobile Heaven

With the invention of the mobile phone,
Which today more and more people own,
We can text messages far and near,
In all different tones ringing loud and clear,
We talk to our friends for hours on end,
Without our phones we'd go round the bend.
But in this world of conveniences mod,
How many of us contact God?
In fact the only stars we see,
Are those appearing on TV.
Ready to grasp at a moment's glory,
Trying to write their own life story.
In this generation never have we,
Achieved so much materially,
Or lost so much to the powers of evil,
With goodness overshadowed by the devil.
If you don't want taken in by the deceiver,
On God's mobile phone just lift the receiver,
No number is needed night or day,
He'll listen to what you have to say.
Get back to the simple things of life,
Where God's inner voice tells you what is right,
In fact you can chat with Him for ages,
And you won't even need the yellow pages!
He'll fix a crisis willingly,
With 999 emergency,
To His Heavenly mobile you can go,
At times when you are feeling low.
And if today you're one degree under,
Just dial His retrieval number,
So here's a text message from God to you -
"Hello my friend, how do you do,
To find out what I have to say,
Please get in touch immediately,
For I know all your hopes and plans,
And your life story is in my hands,
And I will be your guiding star,
My friend no matters where you are.
So take a tip from mobile heaven,
And contact me 24/7."

𝒴

He Holds the Future

In God's Kingdom we'll be clothed in His beauty,
Arrayed in perfection divine,
When we see Him in all of His glory,
Through our souls His radiance will shine.

For each one of our lives He has nurtured,
In this world of sorrow and pain,
But in heaven He holds the future,
And with love and faithfulness reigns.

The poor and the weak and the hungry,
From His heavenly Kingdom He'll feed,
And this will cost us nothing,
For God will supply every need.

By the plight of this world we've been shaken,
By suffering, famine and war,
In His kingdom God's love is victorious,
And we will find peace evermore.

And the scars left by our separation,
Will be healed in His kingdom above,
And we'll rise to meet our loved ones,
On His open wings of love.

But what will He do with the people,
Who to this world's needs have been blind?
Perhaps they'll be last in His Kingdom,
And never its true beauty find.

Face to Face

If we look beyond heaven's shadowed mirror reflection,
We'll find God's image has replaced our own,
Through eyes of faith our vision becomes clearer,
As we communicate with Him alone.

It is not until we see the revelation,
Of Christ that we will fully understand,
When on the sinking sands of life we drifted,
He held us in the hollow of his hand.

As from our eyes the earthly veil is lifted,
And love's pure light shines forth from Heaven's heart,
Then face to face with Christ in all His glory,
We will proclaim "My God How Great Thou Art."

Between the two of us

Lord, just between the two of us, do you not agree?
It's so hard to communicate, when your face I cannot see!
Each time I try to find you, though I search with all my might,
Your whereabouts elude me, for you're hidden from my sight.

And, just between the two of us, when we play 'Hide and Seek',
I think I know just where you are - perhaps I'll take a peek -
You're standing right beside me, only you don't make a sound,
But I've got a funny feeling that your love is all around.

You've found a place within my heart, for your Holy Spirit's there,
And, just between the two of us, I know how much you care,
Together we are partners, my life you understand,
For every corner that I turn, my pathway you have planned.

Some day when I reach Heaven, the 'Game of Life' will end,
And I will come in contact with 'My Very Special Friend',
And just between the two of us, when your face at last I see,
For a lifetime's love and faithfulness - I'll thank you personally!

Broken Wings

There is no hunger or disease
In heaven on high,
But how can a bird on broken wings
Ever reach the sky?
The hungry children without food
Are starving day by day,
Lord heal this needy world of ours,
And help us find our way.

There is no pain or suffering
In heaven on high,
But what about the children
Far too weak to even cry?
There's no destruction by the bomb,
There is no price to pay,
Lord help us see each other's needs,
And then we'll find a way.

The 'Dove of Peace' must fly across
This troubled world of ours,
Bringing healing on His wings,
And spiritual powers.
Lord mend the brokenness and pain
And give us eyes to see,
And then we'll reach the sky again
On wings of majesty.

Sea Pictures of Heaven

There in His secret world under the sea,
God creates miracles for you and me,
Priceless the treasures that He has stored there,
Kaleidoscope jewels and sea pearls so rare.

What are the pictures He's painted below?
In creation's colours as deep waters flow,
Sea pictures of Heaven you will find there,
Protected by nature and God's loving care.

Wondrous creatures in the depths you will find,
Exotic plantation and fish of all kinds,
Beautiful shells on the coral reefs grow,
Dependant on God in their sea world below.

Hidden from view in beauty so rare,
Sea pictures of Heaven beyond compare,
Forever more God's secrets will keep,
In His wonderful world below waters deep.

Just Beyond Your Tears

I've shared a life-time's love with you,
Throughout many years,
But Heaven is not beyond the clouds,
It is just beyond your tears -
Just beyond your tears my love,
Please do not weep for me,
I am still with you as you grieve,
Each falling tear I see.

Do you know that I am near you
Every moment of the day,
For heaven is not beyond the clouds,
It is just a breath away -
Just a breath away my love,
Parted for just a while,
Remember in God's precious time,
Again you'll see my smile.

Your loving heart beats close to mine,
As you live from day to day,
For heaven is not beyond the clouds,
It is just a beat away -
Just a beat away my love,
Even though you are bereft,
Everlasting love we'll find once more,
And it will conquer death.

My Eternal Dream

I have a very special dream of heaven,
More beautiful than I can comprehend,
Reaching beyond this world into eternity,
From earth to heaven above my soul ascends.

And dwelling there amidst eternal beauty,
My Lord and Saviour waits to welcome me,
With arms outstretched in love He bids me welcome,
To paradise - and then His face I see.

What joy as I behold my Lord and Saviour,
His eyes of love look down upon my face
Then with my loved-ones I am re-united,
In Heaven's home I'm sanctified by grace.

The little children gather round the Master,
As He gently lifts each one upon his knee,
And I can hear Him telling them a story,
His smile of love is there for all to see.

And then I hear a million voices singing,
A wondrous song of joy unto the Lord,
Praising the Lord in holy adoration
Worshiping Him in heaven's home above.

Lord hold my special dream just for a life time,
And keep it safely in tranquillity,
Until the moment comes when up in heaven,
I live my dream for all eternity.

Heaven's Dwelling Place

If you could follow me to Heaven's Dwelling Place,
You'd find that it is just beyond your tears,
For in that moment when I passed from death to life,
I heard my Saviour whisper "do not Fear -
For I have prepared a place for you beyond compare,
My beloved one in whom I am well pleased,
Come enter into the living presence of the Lord,
From pain and suffering you are released."

And standing in the presence of the Holy One,
I felt His healing touch of love divine,
And safe in Jesus' arms I am restored again,
In paradise eternal life is mine.
God knows your grief and sorrow and He feels your pain,
For heaven is just one single breath away,
Because love is everlasting we will meet again,
With joy your sorrow Jesus will repay.

One day you'll follow me to Heaven's Dwelling Place,
Where love will triumph over grief and pain,
And just beyond your tears you'll find I'm waiting there,
In Christ we'll be united once again.
And Jesus will reach out and place your hand in mine,
Together we will walk beside the Lord,
For in eternity we'll never part again,
Forever in the Dwelling Place of God.

Sunrise Road

In night's ethereal glow,
Purple and violet shadows
Obscure the moon,
Heaven's stars are distant,
Darkness overtakes the soul,
The earth is the Lords.

Beyond the darkest night lies Sunrise Road,
Crimson, gold and orange light the dawn,
The mirror-image clouds glide slowly by,
Illuminating Heaven's vision,
Arrayed in eternal beauty,
And everlasting glory.

Following the high winding path,
Through silver mirage mountains and hidden valleys,
I draw nearer and nearer to Heaven.
Mystical palm trees sway in the wind,
Where floral blossoms in profusion grow,
Listen, I hear the sound of distant music.

A song of welcome echoes from on high,
Birds of the air soar towards the heavens,
Following ascension's call,
The crystal river of life
Flows from the Holy City,
Bathed in the golden light of God.

Holy angels, arrayed in purest white,
Fly on sacred wings towards infinity,
Bearing my soul to heaven,
With rapture I behold the face of God!
And Heaven's glory is revealed
On Sunrise Road.

Y

The In-between

My Child,
At this moment in time you have reached the in-between,
And I am there,
You do not have to walk this road alone!
I see your unshed tears of sorrow and pain,
And the innermost feelings of your heart,
As you journey through the unknown abyss,
I will walk beside you and never forsake you.

The road in-between is not easy,
But I am there,
Gently healing your tears,
Turning your despair into hope,
And standing in the shadows I will be waiting,
To lead you through the darkness,
Into light.

I will go with you in the in-between,
And together we will take one step at a time,
I will lift you when you stumble,
And hold you in the hollow of my hand,
Raising you through love inseparable,
To find a new dawn,
For joy cometh in the morning.

Y

God's All Revealing Light

My heart in deepest darkness lay,
Broken and torn along life's way,
The sunrise I could not behold,
Shadows obscuring purest gold.

Tears of compassion fell like dew,
And cleansed my soul, Lord was it you?
Did I not feel your healing touch?
Restoring grace I need so much.

And then God's all-revealing light,
Dispelled darkness, restored sight,
And looking through God's eyes of love,
New beauty shone from heaven above.

The sunrise clothed in purest gold,
Creation's touch I did behold,
The glory of the Lord revealed,
To such as me, and I believed.

Tapestry of Paradise

Creator of the Universe,
And all that you have made,
How have you fashioned Paradise,
In colours bright arrayed?
What work of art have you performed?
What masterpiece divine?
Surpasses the beauty of the earth,
By creation's power sublime.

Creator of the Universe,
And all that is to be,
What wondrous colours un-revealed,
That as yet our eyes can't see?
Have you a Heavenly Tapestry
In your vast and mighty plan?
Rivalling the world below,
And the artistry of man?

Creator of the Universe,
As your Kingdom you prepare,
Colour your love and holiness
In Technicolor there,
Colour our lives with loveliness,
That they may ever be
Woven into your tapestry,
In Paradise Lord with thee.

𝖄

Conversion
Hebrews 11 V.1

Standing on the threshold of the world,
My life in the balance – win or lose – which is it to be?
Soundlessly the past recedes,
And future waits to bring me through the night.

As moonlight glances through the storm-ridden clouds,
I reach beyond the darkness
And feel the warmth of your touch upon my face,
Suddenly the peace of God surrounds my soul.

My heart responds –
Transformed by new heights of awareness,
As love so deep, so wide, so high,
Encompasses my inner being.

In the wake of the morning, faith enters -
I make a life-changing decision to cross the threshold,
And walk with God towards a brand new day,
Sure of things hoped for, and certain of what I do not see.

Prayer

Wedding Prayer
(Unspoken Trinity)

In holy reverence we stand within God's dwelling place,
Upon our wedding day our marriage vows we now
embrace,
And from this moment on, our hearts will beat as one,
For love's unspoken trinity we've found in you alone.

The bond of human love, today oh Lord is ours to share,
Each heart string of our lives is touched with joy beyond
compare,
Upon our wedding day, we come to seek your face,
Make of our sacred union Lord a sacrament of grace.

In love's unspoken trinity, and in your guiding hands,
We place our marriage Lord, our future hopes and plans,
Upon this day of days, we dedicate our lives,
And pray God's love we'll always see through one-another's
eyes.

**Our hearts will beat as one, from depths of love divine,
In knowing I am yours, and knowing you are mine.**

Love's Fulfilment

This is your special wedding day,
And love is everywhere,
The scent of bridal blossom,
Leaves its fragrance on the air.
The harmony of piano,
And a haunting violin,
The expression of each other's love,
Which comes from deep within.

Surrounded by the blessing,
Of friends and family,
Waiting for the marriage ceremony,
With great expectancy.
To-day in love's fulfilment,
You will become as one,
Standing before the altar
Now life's journey has begun.

As you come into God's presence,
Your marriage vows to make,
The language of each human heart,
Will of God's love partake.
Pledging yourselves to one another,
As you exchange your wedding rings,
In marriage joined together,
What joy this moment brings.

Now the wedding veil is lifted,
And you are man and wife,
Looking through the eyes of love,
Two hearts as one unite.
And in that special moment,
Reach out and hold God's hand,
And trust Him for the future,
With all your hopes and dreams and plans.

One Moment!

Won't you take one moment!
As you begin another day,
To talk to the Master,
Your faithfulness He will repay.
For precious moments last forever, ever and ever,
And every passing day He'll treasure,
Each moment with you.
One moment!
He'll walk with you the whole day through.

Won't you take one moment!
As the busy world goes hurrying by,
To talk to the Master,
For on His strength you can rely.
For precious moments last forever, ever and ever,
And every passing day He'll treasure,
Each moment with you.
One moment!
His faithfulness will see you through.

And throughout your lifetime,
He'll walk beside you all the way,
Do you think one moment!
Is enough to spend with Him today?
For precious moments last forever, ever and ever,
And every passing day He'll treasure,
Each moment with you.
One moment!
A life-time's love He's given you!

Y

Irish Poems

Erin's Isle

On Erin's Isle beside the emerald mountains,
Where fiddlers play their haunting melodies,
Lilting and sweet the sound of Island music,
Echoes from Irish harps across the seas.

To jigs and reels we danced on Erin's Island,
The pipes of Pan and Irish fluters played,
Those tales of folklore hearts and minds beguiling,
Casting a magic spell 'till break of day.

The love affair we had I still remember,
The treasured moments shared for just a while,
You stole my heart, bewitching me forever,
And most of all I long for Erin's Isle.

Softly the echoes drift across the ocean,
Where Irish harps still play enchantingly,
From Erin's Isle her gentle voice is calling,
Beckoning me across the Irish Sea.

I will return again to Erin's Island,
As Irish melodies the fluters play,
Her magic charms once more my heart beguiling,
Welcoming me forever there to stay.

Vision by Moonlight

Dancing by moonlight in nocturnal beauty,
Never a vision so nymph-like and fair,
Soft Irish pipes in the distance are calling,
Beguiling the maiden with long flowing hair.

Feather-like feet dance to soul haunting music,
Under her spell all nature is still,
Willowy creature in final abandon,
Emerald eyes with mystery fill.

In silhouette like a bright golden halo,
Moonlight caresses this vision in green,
Kisses her lips with consuming passion,
Steals her away never more to be seen.

Y

Faerie Dance

Dance Irish maiden dance, stepping on faerie feet,
Dance to the pipes of Pan, interpreting every beat,
Dance to the Irish harp, hair flowing wild and free,
Dance in a faerie ring, to a mystical melody.
Dance to an Irish jig, gliding on faerie toes,
Turning and circling around, graceful and light she goes,
Dance to the Irish harp, hair flowing wild and free,
Dance in a faerie ring, to a mystical melody.

.Dance Irish maiden dance, rocking on faerie feet,
Dance to the violin, haunting and clear and sweet,
Dance in a reverie, intimate spirit soar,
Casting a magic spell, legend of love and lore.
Dance to an Irish jig, gliding on faerie toes,
Turning and circling around, graceful and light she goes,
Dance in a reverie, intimate spirit soar,
Casting a magic spell, legend of love and lore.

Dance Irish maiden dance, tapping on faerie feet,
Hornpipe and jig and reel, echoing every beat,
Dance to the magic flute's soft lilting melody,
Follow your faerie dream, spirit of ecstasy.
Dance to an Irish jig, gliding on faerie toes,
Turning and circling around, graceful and light she goes,
Dance to the magic flute's soft lilting melody,
Follow your faerie dream, spirit of ecstasy.

Other

God's Windows

Lord, don't clean your windows too early,
Leave them dirty as long as you can,
'Till I've finished me wee cup of coffee,
And smoked the wee fag in me han.

Lord, don't clean your windows too early,
Till I've looked at page three in 'The Sun',
Oh! I've found this wee bit of scandal,
Hold on Lord while next door I run.

Perhaps you could start with the back ones,
While I have a wee gossip or two,
Don't use too much soap in the water,
Sure a lick and a promise will do.

Don't forget to take a wee tea break,
Then maybe I might get a chance,
To bring back this dress for a refund,
Which I wore at the Church's barn dance.

Put your chamois back in your bucket,
While I call and collect the dole,
Sure I could get a wee job in Belfast,
And you might not notice at all!

Continue the job for one hour Lord,
There's a prayer meeting on in the hall,
And then I'll not mind if you see me
With my bible, my hymn book and all.

I think you should stop for to-day Lord,
I've got somethin else in me head,
For this evening I've got to play 'Bingo'
Just wait till tomarra instead.

A Mother's Love

A mother's love is God's most precious gift to the world,
It is unconditional,
Unselfish and all-embracing,
Her kiss can heal bumps and bruises,
And broken hearts.
With her embrace,
She is ready to give you
Hope, sympathy and encouragement,
Is not judgemental,
And never asks for anything in return.
She lends a listening ear
When you are in trouble,
Her words of wisdom are priceless,
Like jewels rare.
When you fall she is there
To give you love and protection,
Until you are ready to begin again.
Her heart cries when you cry,
Over-brims with joy when you are happy,
Swells with pride when you are successful,
Knows great sadness when you cannot find your way,
She is prepared to stand beside you, come what may,
Prays for you day and night,
And holds you in her arms forever.

Making a Difference

The ordinary people who make a difference in this world,
Have a very special story to be told,
Each day their lives speak volumes in an unobtrusive way,
Their kindly deeds all come from hearts of gold.

By just a simple act of love they brighten up your day,
And somehow bring new hope back to your eyes,
You'll find them sympathising in a special kind of way,
These 'ministering angels' in disguise.

A listening ear they'll offer to someone in despair,
Alleviating problems and fears,
Making a conscious effort to show someone that they care,
Like a ray of sun their smile shines through your tears.

With courage and with faith they face each moment of their
lives,
Where God's influence has left His mark of love,
And somehow they are able to turn another page,
And find the goal in life they're worthy of

It really doesn't matter if you're a beggar or a king,
To these people you encounter day by day,
For ordinary people make extraordinary friends,
And they really 'make a difference' on life's way.

Loneliness

What is loneliness?

A broken reed drowning at the edge of life's abyss,
Left to the mercy of the uncaring world,
The curse of indifference at others hurled,
Isolated and lost within the limits of my mind,
Reaching out for long lost happiness I cannot find,
Upon the sinking sand of deep despair,
Never to find someone who really cares,
Facing the inescapable darkness of the night,
Chilled by desolation, is nothing going right?
Like icicles dark shadows grip my soul,
Feelings of loss are struggling to control.

Then suddenly from hidden depths below,
Tears well up, and in their healing flow,
Sorrow's tide begins to ebb away,
And in its wake I face another day,
Surfacing upon the sea of pain,
On reality's shore,
My life begins again,
I look and find new footprints in the sand,
True compassion reaches out to take my hand,
As buried feelings answer to love's touch,
I turn and find the friend I need so much.

Two Hearts as One

From one tiny seed of life we grew,
Inside our mother's womb,
Two little hearts beating as one,
Two little minds in tune,
Side by side each life was formed,
Together right from the start,
Born so alike in every way,
Unable to tell us apart.

In babyhood years we were so close,
As children we played together,
Held by that bond which would always be,
Between the two forever,
Two little hearts beating as one,
Two little minds in tune,
Identical twins from the moment that we,
Were formed in our mother's womb.

The years quickly passed and my twin and I
Grew up and were still together,
With that special bond between the two,
Just as strong and firm as ever,
Knowing each other's secret thoughts,
Each heart and mind as one,
Still feeling that special closeness,
Shared before we were born.

Through life we both have families,
And little grandchildren of our own,
Our two hearts are still beating as one,
As closer we have grown,
Identical twins together,
To each other we relate,
Held by that unbroken love bond,
Which nothing can separate.

My twin sister and I are identical and she is my 'forever friend'.

Imprints

God has given you the gift of life,
To cherish and to share,
What are the imprints you will leave on this world,
Showing people that you care?
Will the marks that you make be remembered
By your fingerprints of love?
Touching the heart of each person you meet,
With blessing from above.

Do you hold the hands of your children,
With love and with sympathy?
Do your fingers leave an imprint
For life on your family?
Each hug they'll remember forever,
As they journey along life's way,
Holding the hands of the Master,
As you live from day to day.

And what about your footprints?
Do you go the extra mile?
Are you prepared to walk through life
With courage and a smile?
Following the steps of the Master
Where Jesus' feet have trod,
Leaving a permanent imprint,
On the road that leads to God.

The path of life is difficult,
Take one step at a time,
Helping those less fortunate,
As the uphill road you climb,
Leaving God's imprint behind you,
Faithful in all that you do,
Following Jesus' footprints,
Wherever He takes you to.

Y

The Woman of the Well

As I stood beside the well, everybody passed me by,
I was lonely, and was going who knows where?
In the shadow of the sun, a stranger sat alone,
And He asked me for a drink as I stood there.

He looked into my eyes and He seemed to realise
That my broken dreams had no reality,
In the shadow of the sun, it was Jesus who had come,
And had spoken to a woman such as me!

"Fear not my child, said He, for I will give to thee
'Living Water' which will satisfy your soul!"
All my burdens and my cares I gave to Jesus there,
And His 'Living Water' cleansed and made me whole!

I'm the woman of the well, and my story I will tell,
Jesus satisfied the thirst within my soul!
He set my spirit free from the sins that shackled me!
And His 'Living Water' cleansed and made me whole!

Come with me to the well, and meet with Jesus there,
There was nothing in my life He could not see,
My virtue was restored in the presence of the Lord!
By the 'Living Water' freely given to me!

y

He Touched My Soul

I looked for God with eyes that could not see,
He touched my soul, as He looked back at me,
His love was there, beyond compare,
He touched my soul! He touched my soul!
As He stood there I felt His touch divine,
His unseen love reached to this soul of mine,
Oh God of Love, you made the blind man see,
Oh may I find your look of love for me.

I prayed to God there was a veil between,
He touched my soul as He stood there unseen,
His love was there, beyond compare,
He touched my soul! He touched my soul!
As He stood there I felt His touch divine,
His unseen love reached to this soul of mine,
Oh God of Love, you made the blind man see,
Oh may I find your look of love for me.

God give me grace, although I cannot see,
His arms reached down, and they encompassed me,
His love was there beyond compare,
He touched my soul! He touched my soul!
As He stood there I felt His touch divine,
His unseen love reached to this soul of mine,
Oh God of Love, you made the blind man see,
And now I've found your look of love for me.
He Touched My Soul.

This is my personal testimony

𝒴

Lightning Source UK Ltd.
Milton Keynes UK
UKOW051417011011

179578UK00001B/51/P